The Dharma of Marriage

A Life Practice

by
Michael Erlewine

ISBN-10:
1516970543
ISBN-13:
978-1516970544

Lots of free e-books at DharmaGrooves.com

Michael@Erlewine.net

Table of Contents

The Dharma of Marriage 4
Introduction 4
Divorce 10
Karma 11
Intent 11
Aggression 11
Victim 12
Balance 12
The Dharma of Marriage 16
The Problem with Marriage 20
Marriage: The Most Common Form of Yoga 26
Love and Compassion 30
Reaction Tong-Len: The Alchemy of Reactions 36
    The Kinds of Meditation 36
    Meditation Hurdles 37
    Practice Places 38
    Karma 38
    Micro-Karma 39
    The Self 40
    Reaction Toning 41
    Imprint or Groove 42
Sending & Receiving: Tong-Len 45
Tong-Len: How I Came to Learn It 49
Response Ability 54
Reactive Alchemy 57

Podcast up to page 16:

http://spiritgrooves.libsyn.com/the-dharma-of-marriage-and-relationshiips-237

The Dharma of Marriage

A Life Practice

Tibetan Buddhist monks and laypersons, along with Zen Buddhist, have developed methods of training the mind that are over 1,000 years old and have proved very effective. These amount to a life-long practice. Marriage for many of us is also a life-long practice just as difficult and complete as many dharma practices. This article is about using these tried and true dharma practices within a marriage to solve problems and to help keep it together.

Introduction

The outer signs of marriage include the legal document for the state and usually some form of ceremony, but those are just the external signs of marriage. As many religions point out, marriage is a sacrament, meaning that it is sacred, and whatever makes it sacred is what causes two people to marry. In other words (and IMO), what is more important is an inner event that happens before the marriage ceremony takes place.

I am not saying that in this modern world that every marriage is triggered by a deep internal event, because the divorce rate would suggest otherwise. It is my belief that many divorces could be avoided with just a little remedial mind-training. In these articles I am only concerned with marriages that come from some kind of deep (and spiritual) discovery, shared by two individuals, like the act of falling in love.

I can't speak for young people today, but in the world I came up in (1950s-1960s) finding someone to love (and falling in love) was on just about every young person's mind. As for marriage, we all knew or assumed that true love led to union or its equivalent legal form of marriage.

4

I spent many years searching through this world (and wondering after every young woman I met) to see if she was "the one." I was afraid that a moment's inattention on my part and she might slip by me unnoticed. When I finally met my wife, I immediately understood that could never have happened, because there is no way I could have avoided her, and that is because falling in love does not come from outside us, but from within. We have it within us and it happens when it happens, not to say that I think of it as a game of musical chairs.

There are just a few main points in this article that I want to make and one of them is to say something about falling in love. There apparently are different levels of love, but a general axiom might be: if you have questions as to whether this current person you are infatuated with is the one for you to marry, chances are that he or she is not the one. Keep going, because real love imprints itself on us such that there is no doubt. After all, that is what falling head over heels in love is all about. Among other things, when we meet our destined partner, any uncertainty is lost. We become, as they say, starry-eyed.

In my own case, as a prominent local musician on the Ann Arbor, Michigan scene, I had many opportunities to meet women. And women seem to like musicians. Even so, I did not jump at just "any" opportunity, but was rather selective. Of course, the sad part is that I had never been in love to the point of marriage, so I was kind of feeling my way along here. After having finally met my wife Margaret, I then knew (in hindsight) that falling in love was nowhere near as subtle as I had imagined it might be; I was just shy. After all, marriage is intimate, intimate beyond imagination as those of us who are married well know.

Nor was finding the right woman for me as simple as adding up attributes on a checklist to see who has the highest total, not that I ever really did that, but there was

5

something like that going on, checking girls out. There was a bit of the "Eeny-Meeny-Miny, Moe" every once in a while.

Actually meeting Margaret was more like being hit with a sledge hammer as far as impact goes, but, of course, much nicer. It seems that Mother Nature is not subtle in this department, and that she takes no chances. Guesswork on my part was not needed, because falling in love is a life changer. Even a little thought beforehand would have told me that, but I never thought about it that way until after I had experienced it.

And I had been in love before or at least infatuated, and as great as that was, it was remarkably different from what happened when I met Margaret. For one, all of my infatuations lacked the overriding sense of compassion that I felt with Margaret or my desire to care for them personally. We were not one, but more like me over here and them over there – two separate people.

The marriage vows that we recite publically and that are taken so seriously by society are, themselves, just a sign and signature of a much deeper experience that has already taken place deep within us before the ceremony. The day of our actual wedding, while nice, was logistically (and otherwise) somewhat of an ordeal.

And, as painful as it might be to hear, my advice is that if you have not fallen in love enough to change your life forever, then you may not have fallen in love yet. Infatuation is strong too.

I used to think that falling in love was when two people merge and become One, but after the experience of actually falling in love I would now rephrase that: two people together realize that they are already "One," one love and two people. This can be a subtle distinction, but I spell it out for you in more detail later in my own account of meeting Margaret.

After some fifty years as a counseling astrologer, what most of my clients ask and care about is love, relationships, and marriage, almost every one, and especially ladies. Men are a little more shy.

What is remarkable through all those years of working with people and listening in extreme detail to their relationship stories is that almost all relationships have problems and the problems are almost always the same problems. Everyone seems to have them, and they don't just scratch the surface, but dig deep grooves in the relationship that are not easy to solve or remove. Yet I believe most of the problems can be resolved, with some effort. If you believe that solving the problems in a marriage should be as easy as falling in love was and getting married, guess again.

And my next statement will most probably not be appreciated, but I offer it just the same. Although many couples trying to save their marriages that I counseled sought out various forms of therapy and counselors, that therapy, while useful at first, in the long run petered out and was eventually abandoned, and I will tell you why.

It is not because the therapist was not qualified, although from some stories the therapist were more messed up than their clients, but because ultimately someone else cannot solve what only we can solve for ourselves. And I have an actual dislike for those therapists who end up habituating their clients to their services, so they become hooked like addicts. Avoid them is my advice.

The true counselor or therapist, IMO, is there to provide methods that their clients can use to work on themselves, and none of the methods I am aware of should take more than a session or two to explain to someone. Again, that is just my experience. I am not saying there are not good therapists out there, but I believe they are rarer than people imagine.

In my own case, and I have been married for going on 44 years, the only methods of resolving marriage problems I have found that are actually useful, at least for me, are the ancient mind-training methods of the Tibetan Buddhists. They actually work, and they will be the methods I share with you here. I am not saying not to go to therapists and counselors, but if you go, it will take more than talk to solve your problems, and IMO the money spent and time taken to have endless therapy are much better spent working on yourself and saving that money.

In other words, I am not offering you therapy here, but just presenting a method that is over 1,000 years old and has been vetted and found sound. I have spent over forty years studying, practicing, and working with Tibetan Buddhist methods of mind training, and this includes most of the traditional practices, beginning, middle, and advanced. Marriage has all of the components of a true dharma practice (or very close), although marriage is a difficult form of practice because it involves two practitioners and there is a lot at stake, like: the marriage.

However, if your marriage is already rocky and both partners are willing work at it, these Tibetan mind-training methods actually work, but it will take real work on your part. If only one partner is willing to work on the problem (and the other uninterested), it still can be done, but it is proportionally more difficult. It is kind of an oxymoron to consider solving marriage problems with only one partner. It takes two to tangle, and two to untangle.

A popular myth with newlyweds is that the two of you are going to work side by side at the same task, like a synchronized swim team. This sometimes happens, but not as often as you might think because, aside from sharing love and life, a couple still consists of two persons, and two personalities. And these personalities were made separately, before meeting one another, and they can be very different – backgrounds, upbringing, etc. Yes, when push comes to shove, we work side by side to stem the tide, but left to our own devices, we can naturally drift apart into what is appropriate to our personality, upbringing, and lifestyle. And they usually differ. Pretending they should be the same is an exercise in futility.

What "is" shared is the mutual concern for each other, caring and treating your partner as you would your self, and putting their interest on a par with your own or even ahead of your own. This is something that should have been naturally imprinted when you fell in love, since that is what falling in love is all about, suddenly finding that another person is already sharing your world, a common life and sense of unity; the two are found to be one. In other words, marriage results from the first time that you discover that you care for another person as much as you do for yourself.

We also discover, soon after we are married, that the intimacy we have with our spouse cuts both ways. We have no secrets, but we also have openly shared our weaknesses, including all the buttons that no one else knows how to push. But our partner does, and when things get edgy or go south, those buttons can get pressed and we have little to no defense.

I can't think of a better or more complete situation for a effective dharma practice than a real marriage, one sealed by openness between partners, which is what true love entails. In effect, we are already alone together with our loved one, literally in the same boat. Basically everything is shared including our weaknesses. I can't find the quote, but there is an anecdote to the effect that a Buddhist monk who had completed all of the dharma practices his lama gave him and got passing grades. And his teacher says to him, and now for your final and most difficult practice, meet your wife to be."

So those of us who are married have married into one of the most impossibly demanding dharma practices ever invented, so we are going to need all of the dharma techniques we can master. Marriage is like that and facilitates everything good on the upside, but when things flip around, the same openness makes each partner most vulnerable to the other. In other words, we know how to love each other, but also just how to hurt each other, and when forced to, at times can and will do that.

Divorce

Divorce is not only difficult, even mentioning it tends to bring out the worst in some people. My view is that marriage is irreversible and that you can't put the toothpaste back in the tube. I am not saying that divorces should never happen or that divorcees cannot find true love. Not at all.

What I am saying is that the realization that leads to marriage cannot be walked back into what we were before we fell in love and got married. As mentioned, a virgin is only a virgin once, and an unmarried person who marries cannot marry again for the first time. I consider a divorced person as married, but at present not to anyone they know. The realization that led being married cannot be taken back, so IMO the divorcee is a special state of mind, neither single again nor married. A painful analogy would be a parent who has lost a child. Something has changed that cannot be undone. Enough said. We don't have to agree on this.

Many people seek to justify their divorce in any way they can imagine. We all know that divorce is common, and sometimes it is a good thing. My point is that divorce might be avoided if the couple would learn some basic methods of clearing up their vision, which affects how they see and respond to one another. And a second point is that I have

1

seen many couples who have done no remedial work, divorce, and take their problems to the next relationship and do the same thing all over again – a downward spiral.

The bottom line is that no matter how many existential situations we may describe that are detrimental to a relationship, the remedy or antidote to these problems is always developing greater awareness of the situation until we can take advantage of ways to improve it. This is the value of these Buddhist mind-training techniques that have been used, as I mentioned, for over 1,000 years. This is not something that I just made up.

Karma

We need to talk about karma and its accumulation. Some of you don't know this term or are not comfortable with it, since it may sound strange and foreign, which of course it is. I am going to use the word, and I will define as best I can. Feel free to find your own words for this term and use them.

The Buddhist concept of karma is easy to understand. Every action we make has an effect or reaction. That is simple physics. What is different with the laws of karma from simple physics is that karma also takes note of the "intent" of our every action and factors that in. There is "good" and "bad" karma, positive and negative. We accumulate both. Here I am looking at just the "bad" karma, the karma we accumulate that adds up and further obscures our mind so that we become less and less aware. That is what is "bad" about bad karma. Karma, as mentioned, has everything to do about intent.

And it this "intent" that I want to draw your intention to here, as it relates to marriage and our marriage partner. If we want to protect our marriage and to not stain the initial realization that led to it, we have to careful about the intent of our actions toward our partner, obviously, especially when we are at odds. Our bad intent creates karma that only further obscures the clarity of our relationship. Both partners are advised about their intent, and if it is off the mark, then it can be purified and the stains it creates gradually removed.

It is just like doing the laundry. Our new clothes don't just stay new if we wear them. They can get dirty and we have to wash them to keep them clean. It is no different with our relationship. If we want clean clothes, we have to get out those stubborn stains. In a relationship, if we want clear sailing, we have to straighten out what gets bent. There are mind training methods just for this.

Intent

As mentioned, one important consideration is our "intent," what the intent was for a given action. Two people can break a rare ceramic plate, one without meaning to and the other intending to smash it. The plate is broken either way, but the karma recorded is very different. When it comes to accumulating karma, the teachings say that our intent is everything.

If we intend to use mind training to help stabilize our relationship, then we should examine our intent after every aggressive action, large or small. Becoming aware of our intent can lead to toning that intent down until we are just being open, and not being aggressive. If we can determine that our intent was to hurt or harm, even if only in defense, we should note and acknowledge that and find ways to purify that response.

Aggression

The great Tibetan siddha Chögyam Trungpa Rinpoche said that the opposite of enlightenment was aggression in any form. If we look, we know when we are being aggressive when we are pushing the envelope, even just a tiny bit. That's all it takes for aggression to be felt by our partner, and they may respond in kind and there we go again, round and round. We can monitor our actions as to their aggressive intent. Aggression is basically sadistic, the intent to harm.

Victim

Harder to recognize and control, by nature, is the tendency to become the victim in a situation, to take offense when perhaps none was intended. Western psychologists call this masochism, but we all get our feelings hurt from time to time, get down on our self, and on occasion spiral way downward out-of-control. If this is our tendency, as I mentioned, this is harder to catch ourselves doing than is aggression.

However, if we are vigilant and develop enough awareness, we can stop it right there at the onset, recognize it for the step downward that it is, and just drop it right there. We can say no thank you to depression, inferiority, and all the downers we may be vulnerable to. It is not that we can't go there, but that we have been there, done that, and it doesn't help things.

Balance

Obviously a balance of some kind is needed between being aggressive and being aggressed-upon unnecessarily. Psychologists might call this dichotomy a tendency to sadism or masochism, intending to inflict pain or being too quick to feel vulnerable and be the victim.

Either way, the remedy for this condition begins with developing greater awareness so that we can intercede on behalf of our better nature when we catch ourselves being aggressive or taking offense.

The good motto seems to be that while we cannot control what is incoming, but we can always learn to control our response to either aggression or victimization.

So this boils down to the question of how do we learn to become more aware? Of course, there are many answers to this, just as many as there are mind-training methods. Remember that the word Buddha means "awareness" or perhaps "the one who is aware," so all of the many Buddhist mind-training methods are all about developing our awareness.

I have been working with these methods for more than forty years now and, while I am not enlightened yet, I have learned at least something about the various techniques, how difficult or easy they are to learn, what kind of result we can expect, and in what time frame.

So I am considering the effort it will take you to get up to speed on these mind training techniques, and recommending methods that will not take you forty years as it did me, right? The goal of all mind-training techniques is clearing out obstacles and obscurations so that we can develop awareness easier.

There are no magic mind-training methods. They all, every last one of them, depend upon our individual effort because Buddhism and any enlightenment, if nothing else, is a do-it-yourself project. If the Buddha were here in the room with us, he could not walk over and touch me on the head, and I would be enlightened. What he could do, which is what he did do, is share his method of developing awareness with us, which is called the "dharma." The dharma is a series of mind-training practices that help us to develop greater awareness.

In the case of relationship problems, what we need is enough awareness to see when we are being aggressive toward our partner, or being overly vulnerable and taking on something we will resent later. Both things happen to all of us at one time or another.

If we can see what is going on better, we can learn to respond appropriately to whatever is being thrown at us, instead of reacting impulsively. As those of us who are married well know, reacting impulsively and saying or doing things we don't really mean only further stains a relationship. And it is also true of the opposite, allowing ourselves to become a victim of our partner's aggression. So, there is a lot at stake here.

With enough awareness, we can stop reactions before they happen and, instead, respond appropriately and proportionally to whatever arises. I am not saying this is easy, but it is easier than to continue to react impulsively and further damage the relationship. In other words, it is very much worth learning. And where do we begin?

We begin by learning a Buddhist mind-training technique that is at least 1,000 years old called Tong-Len, and here were are going to start with a form of Tong-Len called "Reaction Tong-Len," also called "Reaction Toning," which just is a method of toning down our impulsive reactions. This is the easiest method of its kind that I know of and, if we are serious about it, we can greatly tone down our reactions and learn to replace them with appropriate responses, ones that will help to preserve the relationship.

All that is needed is that you make enough effort, keep at it, until you can begin to see some results. And the technique is very simple. All that is required is that you begin to note, to be aware of, your own reactions. It does not matter what causes your reactions, where they come from, or what the intent was, but only that when you react, you take note of it and tone it down.

And let's not worry about pleasant reactions, things you like. Instead, concentrate on the ones that make you wince, draw back, and become defensive. It could be as simple as someone who says something that hurts your feelings, or when you run into a person you know doesn't like you, the kind of reaction you have to them. And it does not matter whether that person intends to threaten you or not. It only matters here that you react and how much.

We lose a tremendous amount of energy in reacting negatively to what life brings us. And when we wince or close off our openness, it is like the ostrich that sticks its head in the sand. We lose whatever awareness that we have and go into something like a micro-hibernation for a nanosecond or too. And the saddest thing is that we do this so habitually that we are no longer aware that we are even doing it.

So the first step is to become aware how we react, when we record a reaction. And the effects of these reactions add up and gradually accumulate as an obscuration in our mind. These microseconds of hurt gradually dig a groove in our mindstream that only gets deeper and deeper each time we do it.

The Tibetans point out that we are recording karma with each instance and, as mentioned, these instances add up and are what I call micro-karma. And the teachings tell us that karma always burns twice, once when we record our negative reaction, and twice when somewhere down the road we take steps to remove its effects. And this kind of karma accumulation makes deep-down stains or grooves in our mindstream. Every wince adds up until the load of micro karma that we create each day is greater than most any big mistake we might make in a day.

So the operative thing to do is to develop enough awareness to stop reacting, whereby the tracks of your previously accumulated karma will begin to face out.

The Dharma of Marriage

If you would rather listen to this as a podcast, here it is:

http://spiritgrooves.libsyn.com/the-dharma-of-marriage-235

I thought I was done with this theme, but apparently not. In these blogs, I try to present ideas that I find valuable and that I imagine might be value to you as well. Here is one that is invaluable if you can make sense out of it. It is about why marriage is sacred to us.

In the major forms of Vajrayana Buddhism, which include the Tibetan Buddhist lineages and some of the Zen Buddhist lineages, of course there is the goal of eventual enlightenment. We all know that. What is not so clear is that there is an intermediate stage before enlightenment, when we first get the general idea of how we personally can go about enabling our own enlightenment, and take the first real steps toward it.

This stage is called "Recognition" by the Tibetan Buddhists and "Kensho" by the Zen Buddhists. Recognition is not enlightenment or anything close to it. As its name suggests, it is simply the recognition of the true nature of the mind, or at least a glimpse of it. It is realizing how the mind actually works and, equally important, that you can work it. At the point of recognition we have everything that we need to enlighten ourselves. We just have to do it.

Recognition of the true nature of the mind can really happen only once, because it is just that, a recognition, a form of realization. Sometimes in the tradition the analogy that is used is that of a coiled rope in a room with little light. For all the world the rope looks like a snake, and to someone coming into the room, they actually see a snake. However, once they have a little more light, they see that it is just a piece of rope, That recognition is a realization. A realization is a one-way trip, meaning that once we realize

16

we are looking at a rope, we don't and can't go back to seeing it as a snake. That is what recognition is like. And that is a traditional analogy.

I use another analogy to indicate what recognition is, one that came naturally to me. We have all seen those picture-paintings, where embedded within one picture is another picture, but it is carefully hidden. You can't see it unless it is pointed out. But once it is pointed out, we can always see the hidden picture whenever we look. That is recognition, which is a form of realization.

The great siddhas and mahasiddhas go even further. They say that there are many dharmas and many teachers of those dharmas. But for any one of us, there is only one teacher who will first successfully point out to us the true nature of the mind. And this is called your Tsawi Lama or root guru. It only happens once, because, as I explained, it is a realization and not just another experience or an intellectual understanding.

The teachers and siddhas go on to say that once your root guru has pointed out to you the true nature of the mind, and you have seen it, his or her job is essentially done. At that point you have what you need to proceed on to enlightenment under your own steam, and on a path that only you can know and follow. Hopefully, with these words you can understand what a "Realization" is and why it happens only once. And that's not the end of my message here.

There is one more analogy for you to take in, and it's a doozy. Love relationships are like this, especially the love relationship that leads to full engagement, and then on to marriage. When we meet the one we will marry, we recognize them differently from other relationships that we have had. In fact, this too is a realization, one that can only happen once.

17

And the person with whom we have this realization is the one that was permitted (in this life) to bring us to the recognition that this is the one we want to marry. It can only happen once because, as I have been careful to point out here, it is a recognition (a realization) and not just another one of our relationship experiences.

Of course, some of us will have many lovers and even many marriage partners. That is not what I am pointing at here. I am suggesting that no matter how many lovers you have, there is only one that first brought you to the realization that led to full engagement, which then led to your marriage, just as a virgin is only a virgin once.

If you follow my argument then you know why some faiths don't recognize divorce as a reality. Of course divorce is a legal reality. But you can't un-realize a realization. That is what the Catholic Church is saying when they don't recognize divorce, and this is why divorces are like a third wheel. Along with those who are single and those who are married, there are those who are divorced, but still married in a sense. You can't walk back a realization.

I am not saying that all that passes for engagement, marriage, and divorce in this modern world is pure. But I am saying that if you have had the realization of a beloved that leads to marriage, then that realization is pure, is sacred to you, no matter what happens next or later. You may stay married or you may divorce, but in a very real way the divorcee is still married and always will be. They are no longer a virgin spiritually, so to speak. You can't put the toothpaste back in the tube.

The logic of the above analogy has very little wiggle-room. Of course you are welcome to ignore it, if you can. Yet if you investigate and test this out for yourself, I believe you will agree with me.

So when they say that marriage is a sacrament and is sacred, this view backs that up 100%. With that having been said, if we are married and run on hard times, one of the things we can do is to remember our vows, and the moment in our life when we took them. And here what I mean about vows is not just the words "I do" that occur in most marriage ceremonies, but the rather the "I do" that confirmed the realization that each of us had (or should have had) when we first meet the one who we are destined to marry. For me it was more like "I do. I do. I do." And I did.

As to how this realization of our destined partner can appear, I only have my story to tell, and I told it several blogs back, the one called "Love and Compassion."

Now, before I get a flurry of dissent, I am not saying that everything we know that happens in modern marriages, re-marriages, divorces, and so on does not happen (because it does) or that this is "bad." What occurs to me is that there is an archetype-realization that does happen, just as there is a major realization in the Buddhist mind-training methods called "Recognition." Realization is a permanent imprint in the mindstream, not just another experience.

For myself, I found it very informative to go back to the realization I had when I realized I wanted to marry Margaret, and saw that was still there and very pure. Some 43 years into marriage, the road gets dusty and sometimes dim. What I have found is that the Tibetan mind-training methods are incredibly valuable for removing some of the obscurations and obstacles to a happy marriage, at least ours. Margaret and I both work on removing these obstacles using the Tibetan Buddhist methods every day.

So, let's discuss this, probably-not-so-popular view of mine.

The Problem with Marriage

If you would rather listen to this as a podcast, here it is:

http://spiritgrooves.libsyn.com/the-problem-of-marriage-236

As an astrologer since the 1960s, for many years I made my living doing readings and counseling clients. It is not surprising that I became skilled at those things I was most asked to read a chart about, and at the tip of the top of that list is marriage and relationships, followed close by vocational questions, and then on down the line. By default, relationship problems became something I am familiar with, not to mention that having been married almost 44 years I was bound to learn something.

Since I have been touching on marriage these last couple of blogs, I would be remiss not to acknowledge some of the problems that marriage can bring, because they are certainly there. I mentioned previously the concept that relationship partners can mirror each other perfectly, down to the last detail, and we don't always want to see ourselves in the mirror.

However, one problem with the fact that married partners reflect one another is that these mirrors are not always true. They adapt to our neuroses like those old funhouse mirrors; they bend and warp the images they reflect. It is my confirmed belief that if married partners are having a rough time through mutual criticism, they might consider adopting standard mind-training methods and clean up the mirrors through which they reflect their partner and themselves. If they do this, their arguments should subside, after which exchanges of a critical nature (mutual reflections) would gradually become more useful and less compromising.

It's not that the criticism of one partner for another is not taken in and registered, but that because the criticism is often magnified and distorted (both ways), that the partner receiving the criticism is often moved to ignore it completely. In other words, if there is some truth of a critical nature as to how we see ourselves, if that truth is exaggerated, then it becomes easier to simply dismiss it entirely.

And it is a good question as to whether criticism should always be applied indirectly, often to the point of not even being quite clear enough or whether it should be spoken directly, looking truth in eye. Both ways can hurt. Of course there is a middle way here that must be found. If you have to treat your partner with kid gloves less they blow up, to the point that they never hear you at all and remain in their little cocoon, then that is not going to work out either. On the other hand, if you get in their face overmuch and just threaten or enrage them that too will not work out. This is where the original compassion for each other is important to find again.

The mirroring that takes place between couples, when there is mutual trust, can only improve the relationship. It was what attracted you to one another in the first place. It seems that much of the reception of this reflection depends on the bedside manner in which it is presented. It is hard to receive criticism from someone who you don't trust, or worse, who does not trust you. What you get is a Catch-22, which results in a vicious cycle of accusations and denials. It goes round and round, ridiculously. It is exhausting.

As it is, our own criticism of our self may be too lax or too severe. When criticism comes from our partner inside a relationship such as marriage, then each partner is essentially or at least initially defenseless. We don't see it coming, because it is coming from the inside where we live, rather than from the outside where we are used to filtering the incoming and can defend ourselves.

And finally, it is the recursive-ness of the mirroring that is destructive, when mirroring becomes a hall of mirror-echoes that are out of control and appear endless. All true reflection is lost. And worst, half of what we say even we don't believe is true. The situation is just out of control.

And then there is the one where our past destroys the future. Our partner can always reach farther into the past to find a case or instance where we committed whatever offense that is being spotlighted and say to us "See, you did that!"; since we are guilty, we are therefore guilty forever into the future. We did something that made them lose trust in us back then, therefore they must protect themselves from us now and on into the future. One partner or both may have reasons not to forgive or trust the other anymore, no matter what. This reasoning is particularly insidious and hard to resolve.

What was and should be a delicate balance, a stable relationship, gets way out of line and needs to be recalibrated, but how is that done? When things flare out of control exponentially, when they go from zero to sixty in seconds, how can they be reined in, short of abandoning the nest and marriage entirely, and just starting over?

And giving up and starting over, which can work at times, is not all it's cracked up to be. I love this bit of poetry from the graphic artist Michelangelo that reads:

"What if a little bird should escape death for many long years, only to suffer an even crueler one."

More often than not we jump from the frying pan into the fire, and the next partner we choose exhibits the same problem, only in a cruder form. Having done many, many readings for couples or one-half of a couple, I have seen this happen again and again. The problem is in the client, and they go right out and choose another relationship that is even worse, which brings home to them the problem in a yet harsher form. They would have been better off working it out with their first partner.

And when both parties are inflamed, it can be very difficult to disarm the situation. We see this same phenomenon when two opposing armies attempt to stand down, to lay aside their weapons at the same time... not an easy thing to do.

It's almost like we need to adopt a surgical procedure, the kind of step-by-step methodical care that we see in a hospital. Perhaps we can be kind and loving when we are relating to a third person, but two partners who have escalated a disagreement beyond reason have trouble doing this.

The bottom line for me, the way I see it, is that marital standoffs and internecine wars between couples require the same exact mind-training methods that we would use elsewhere. Until some remedial training is done, the situation will never change enough to be of much help. Both partners have their hands on each other's button and can drop the F-bomb whenever they wish.

The couple needs to consciously work very hard on themselves, and very hard on not reacting to what they find as offensive in and from their partners. I am reminded of the sport of curling where a player slides a granite stone across the ice toward a target while another player sweeps (or does not sweep) the ice, either slowing the stone down or trying to lengthen the distance the stone travels. My reference here is to the intensity of the efforts by the sweepers to move or not to move the stone. This is the kind of attention we have to pay to avoid further staining a relationship. We have to maintain goodwill.

23

If only one partner works on their mind training and the other does not, then it is much more difficult to come to a happy medium, but not impossible. It simply means that the one partner was do double-duty, control their own offense plus control how they respond, because there is no reciprocity. Even if we are unmarried, we are all married to this life, and the resulting relationship is not all that different from a marriage.

Most quarrels between couples are inside jobs; what we freely reveal to someone we trust is later used against us in a court of war. And withholding evidence only makes it worse. It is amazing how the bonds of marriage themselves create a perfect storm for dharma work, a tempest in a teapot, like one of those sealed herbariums that are self-sustaining. It is hard to put the fires out. They smolder.

I could go on for pages, but all of this should be familiar to anyone in a close relationship of a certain duration. I will just mention in passing what I call the "cold wars" that can break out, where there is little to no speaking to one another for hours, days, or longer. And then somewhere down the line one or both partners crack a smile and laughter takes over. Things come back to normal. They can you know.

The more I examine my own marriage and the state of that relationship, the more it is clear to me that marriage should be considered as a major dharma practice, and a complete one at that. Unlike other sadhanas that I have practiced, marriage has the virtue of coming after me if I lapse, and giving me very little quarter at that. I can skip my dharma practice, but I can't skip my marriage. It is always right there reflecting me back at myself.

In May of 1967 I had a major breakthrough in how I viewed life. One of the things that I did at that time is to just walk into the offices of famous or noteworthy people and ask to speak with them about life. Many were just too uptight to allow that, but others were open to it. Perhaps my favorite memory of that time is going into the office of the famous economist Kenneth Boulding, who was only too happy to sit down with me. Together we laughed, cried, and shared our lives. We both read our poems to one another.

And he left me with this piece of advice, that we all are going to fail eventually, but we can learn to fail successfully. Even marriages get old, but they too can age successfully.

Your thoughts?

Marriage: The Most Common Form of Yoga

Marriage is nothing to trifle with. It is some serious stuff. As the ministers often recite during the marriage ceremony, marriage "is not something to be entered into lightly, but rather reverently, advisedly, soberly, and in the fear of God." And I say "Amen" to that.

I like to point out that marriage is the most common form of yoga, which makes those of us who are married, yoga practitioners, and I am not kidding. The word "Yoga" simply means to yoke or join together, unite, which is exactly what marriage does. So I am not joking when I point this out.

If you want to listen to this blog, here is the podcast:

http://spiritgrooves.libsyn.com/marriage-the-most-common-form-of-yoga-234

I understand why there is a civil ceremony for marriage, but I also feel it obscures to a degree the spiritual aspect of marriage, which really is important to recognize and keep in mind. In most cases, marriage reflects a deep inner change, which is what brings marriage about in the first place. Marriage is one of the main rites of passage that many of us go through in life. It is a spiritual event of the first order, and not just a civil occasion.

Those of us who are married may not be trained in meditation or other mind-training methods, but marriage itself is a very rigorous and through training of the mind, one that, as mentioned, is not to be entered into lightly. Marriage, like having children, puts us in a special group or club that those who have not had the experience cannot fully understand or share.

And there is some truth to the Catholic tradition of not allowing divorce. I wouldn't put it that way, but I would say that once marriage vows, like monks vows, are taken, they cannot be easily given back. Divorcees, IMO, exist in a special state of mind and can never go back to actually being single again. Something has changed that does not change back. Even the terminology like "engagement" to be married is pointed.

What exactly is it to be engaged? It sounds to me pretty serious, engagement, and then marriage. As mentioned, I believe there really is no going back, no giving back of the vows once taken, no way of being single again as we were before we were married. There is a difference that remains with divorcees, which I am not going to argue about here, one that those of you who have experienced this, must know.

My point, as mentioned earlier, is that there is more to marriage than a paper certificate. It is not just a civil ceremony, even if you imagine it is. There is a spiritual component that rightly makes marriage sacrosanct, in some way sacred. There is an inner spiritual change that takes place that is profound. The marriage ceremony is an outer sign of an inner transformation.

Marriage happens when two people, two persons, realize that they are already one, already united, "until death do us part," simply because marriage is a realization (or should be), and realizations are forever. They can't be walked back, but are a one-way street.

Use your own words, but those who are married somehow recognize that although they are two people, they are but one being; they are "being together." They are one being (being one) with two personalities, and each partner is responsible for not only their own person, but also for the person of their partner, their "beloved." The dewdrop slips into the shining sea and becomes inseparable. You can't get it back.

And getting married gives way to being married, and that is more than just a continuation of that first inspiration. A marriage has to learn to breathe, which means breathing in and out, up and down, and around. Obviously being married is more difficult than just getting married. The divorce statistics prove this. And this is not to mention the incredible struggles that often go on in most marriages trying to sort out, train, and manage the differences in personalities that are found. I am talking about fights, and they can be ungodly.

I say in all sincerity that marriage itself is a spiritual practice second to none (or equivalent to any), that, as the ceremony invokes, "is not to be entered into lightly." And the same mind-training methods that the Buddha pointed out, which are called the "dharma," are the best methods to use when practicing the yoga of marriage.

It is easy to be generous, civil, kind, and pleasant to a stranger, but incomprehensively more difficult to be so to those closest to us, who can see (and make us see) even the tiniest of our faults in the flawless mirror that marriage presents to us. I see how many dharma practitioners have set up their personal meditation shrine. There is the neatly placed cushion, perhaps a candle or some incense, whatever can create a sense of respect, a special space to practice in.

Our marriage deserves to be treated at least well, at least as special, for it is a practice we do every day, 24x7. There are no holidays from marriage, other than those times when we share its joys. And there is no scarcity of practice, because we practice all day, every day.

I have been married going on 44 years to the same woman, and what I say to myself is: get ready for the long haul. Make your cushion comfortable, light your candle, and clear your mind because marriage deserves all of this, and will require even more from us.

I understand that my words here can but scratch the surface of what is perhaps the most important dharma practice of all, at least for those of us who are married. And we have no choice but to practice, so we might as well practice as best we can and with all our heart.

And the same dharma practices that we do to further our enlightenment, we can bring to our marriage, because there is no difference. Because, in all sincerity, marriage can be (has to be) a complete practice, and it is the most common kind of yoga.

I am sure you have thoughts on this.

Love and Compassion

As a writer I believe that the hardest thing for me to author would be a dictionary. Can you imagine coming up with words to describe that many words? Yet in a way, we each do this internally and here is the problem with that. We use many words that we never even look up, but have just understood by osmosis from the context in which we hear them used around us. And the dangerous part of this is that with some words we end up not with the gist of the word, but perhaps the gist of the gist of the word, or worse just something we imagined it means. We really never sat down and thought it out. For me, the word "Compassion" is one of these.

Of course I know what the word means and use it all the time, but what does it mean? If I really double down on it, I find that my understanding of it does not go very deep. Perhaps it is because compassion is one of those "spiritual" words that I just assume I don't fully understand, although in actuality I must have some compassion in there somewhere, but perhaps working under another name, an alias.

Am I compassionate? Are you compassionate? I am not sure that I have ever stopped to consider what compassion is. If I check the dictionary, it tells me that compassion has to do with "others," someone beyond or other than our self. Actually, the etymology of the word states that compassion means "to suffer with." Perhaps we have compassion when we realize that in this world we all suffer to some degree. I love the etymology of words, but what is even better is when I finally realize by personal experience what the word refers to, when I finally get it.

And I don't like to be told how and to whom I should be compassionate. Instead, I am curious to find out where I am naturally compassionate. It has to be in there somewhere. In my experience, perhaps compassion is when I finally put someone else ahead of (or equal with) myself, but how does that happen? I only have my own story, so of course I'm telling that.

As a child, my first compassionate feelings were for animals and all of the suffering that we find in Mother Nature, where almost every creature struggles to find something to eat and at the same time tries not be eaten. It occurred to me much later to feel compassion for people too, probably because I was not around many that suffered. Even today I sometimes feel I like animals better than people. I can relax around animals and dogs like me.

Probably my first true sense of compassion for others came when I met my wife Margaret, and that is a story, a moment I will never forget. Of course I found her very beautiful, but as a locally-prominent musician I had met all kinds of beautiful women. Back in the day, ladies liked musicians. So how was Margaret different?

When I really contemplate it, perhaps the main difference is in how I responded to Margaret. All those years when I was single, I had been looking through life for someone like myself to love, but a women. I was always afraid I might miss her in the warp and weave of life. I had this idea that the "great being" that I was would someday meet a great being that she was and the two of us would come together and be One. But the reality of meeting Margaret was quite different from that. As the Buddhists point out, expectations seldom are our friend.

I met Margaret in a bar called Mr. Flood's Party in Ann Arbor, Michigan, when I sat down next to her on a barstool and we began talking. There was a little banter, but when that nervousness finally settled down and our eyes locked, something completely else occurred than what I had imagined (or expected) all those years.

I cannot explain why, but as I gazed into Margaret's eyes (and soul) in that noisy barroom I realized, and for the very first time, that there WAS no such thing as two kinds of being or beings, but only the one being, with two kinds of people or persons. In that instant, whatever expectations that I had about the woman that I was searching for all these years vanished, like popping a bubble. It was immediately crystal clear that I had just imagined all of that, made it up. In that first moment of true connectivity I was getting (for the first time) some actual information and it was not as I had imagined it.

The reality, as strange as it may seem, is that I realized (once and for all time) that there is only one "Being," one kind of being. As the great Greek philosopher Parmenides said, "Being alone is," and right then I realized that I had always been alone -- forever. In fact everyone on the planet is alone, yet all together. It has never been any different. What I called loneliness was just my inability to respond to others.

Or, as my dharma teacher pointed out to me, the word "alone" could also be read "All One." This dichotomy I had imagined, that there were two beings that could merge into one, was just another dualism that did not stand up to the reality. I had always been alone together with all other beings.

Summing it up, I realized in that moment that there was, and had been all along, just this one being. In other words, the two separate beings I had imagined, Margaret and I, could never become one because we were already, and had always been, One. We never were two. Now, this may seem to you that I am playing with words here, but there was no abstraction in that moment. This was a realization that has never left me to this very day.

And as to the sense of our "Oneness," Margaret and I, of course, were two personalities, two persons. But my imagined separation or dividing wall between the two of us was not to be found. It just was not there. We were already one. This is what is called by the Buddhists a "realization." It was not something I abstractly understood, nor was it an experience that would come and go over time. No, it was a one-time realization that, once attained, has never changed one iota.

And that moment was "It," my equivalent to the falling in love we all hear about. In that oneness, for the first time in my life, I found myself caring for another person as much as I did for myself. I had let another person into my sacred space. There was no difference between us. Whatever wall there initially was between us as separate persons was recognized and seen to be nil -- no longer there. Never was! Instead, it was one being and two persons. As the Spanish say, "Mi casa es tu casa."

And since I was used to taking care of my own person as well as I could, I suddenly felt the same for Margaret and her person. I responded to her person as I would to my own person. And since she was younger and less experienced in the world, at least in my opinion, I also felt protective of her like I had never felt for anyone before. In fact, I felt that if I did not care for her like I would for myself, that she might not be able to find her way in this tough world we live in and might have a difficult time surviving. I couldn't stand the thought of that, so for the first time I turned aside for another person. Perhaps I was being overly protective, but suddenly I was all about protecting and caring for her.

Always before, in the ladies that I courted, I had walked on. I did not feel personally responsible for them. That was their own business. But with Margaret that all changed in an instant.

And think about this. I had met thousands of people in the world, but never one that I felt responsible enough for to put their wellbeing ahead of or on a par with my own. Of course, I always wished everyone that I met well, but I had never just dropped what I was doing and mixed my responsibilities with those of another. So there was this mixing that took place. How do I interpret all of this?

I feel that the breaking of the seal that separated me (in my mind) from other persons, if it was ever to break, had to start with some one person, and Margaret, for me, was that person. And this moment effectively was the birth of compassion in my life, my first taste of putting another person ahead of or on a par with myself. For me, this was a huge realization.

Because this was such an important event in my life, I want to be clear about it. Was this the "love" that I had searched for all my life? It was, but like all expectations that I have had, my cobbled-together ideas of what love was supposed to be were just what I had made up from what all of the experiences, movies, books, peers, etc. allowed. This must be why the Buddhists suggest we not speculate, not build up expectations, but instead investigate.

I often write that this same phenomenon takes place in learning meditation. Before we finally actually can meditate (and not just practice meditation), our expectations must give way to the actual experience of meditation itself. And in time we realize the difference between our made-up expectations and reality. Our expectations are the first casualty to the real experience.

And I am looking here beyond the physical attraction that I felt for Margaret to something deeper. And the "deeper" is what I am writing about here, that beneath or behind the physical is this infinite sense of responsibility, which actually is compassion. Behind, beneath, and beyond "Love" is compassion. Compassion is the basis of love and it occurs when the imagined duality of the self and the particular other dissolves. A seal is broken. Mixing takes place. What is left is one being that is responsible not only for itself, but for all persons that we let into our heart.

Of course, when Margaret and I started to have children they became part of this inner circle of compassion. We put their welfare ahead of our own. And like the drop of water that falls into a quiet pool, the spreading circles which enclose that drop spread, and include more and more as time goes on. In the same way, compassion starts small and increases over time, including more and more of life within its embrace.

The more our compassion takes hold, the more individuals we feel at least some responsibility for. It no longer has to be just the wife and kids, but whichever people we meet that we somehow feel responsible for.

And of course not all relationships are romantic, so we can extend our responsibility, our ability to respond to others wherever we naturally feel it.

This may seem like a long story to get to this very simple point that beyond any physical attraction in a relationship is the compassion that holds it together.

This is how I find these important words like "Compassion" must be treated, by following them out in our own experience, by defining them ourselves.

Listen to this blog as a podcast:

http://spiritgrooves.libsyn.com/falling-in-love-and-compassion-232

Reaction Tong-Len: The Alchemy of Reactions

Here is an introduction to what in my opinion is the easiest to learn meditation method, called "Reaction Tong-Len" or "Reaction Toning."

The Kinds of Meditation

The kind of mediation practiced by Zen and Tibetan Buddhists is what is called "awareness" meditation, learning to allow the mind to come to rest in awareness -- becoming more aware. But here in America, we basically have one word, "meditation," to cover hundreds of existing mind-training techniques, and most of them are not awareness-oriented.

Meditation methods can be divided into what we might call uppers and downers. Downers relax us and uppers make us more aware. The Buddha's teachings actually combine the two such that we learn to relax or rest in awareness. Buddhist methods are all about awareness, being mindful and becoming more aware -- waking up.

As examples of other kinds of meditation, there are "absorption" meditations, where we go inside or are guided in one way or another – eyes closed. Awareness meditation is typically done with eyes open. And there are literally hundreds of meditation types that are basically relaxation therapies of one form or another.

In fact, meditation for many people simply means learning to relax. There is a somewhat subtle difference between this and the methods Buddha taught which was to learn to relax "as it is," so to speak. However, the Buddha taught to allow the mind to relax and rest in awareness, not in relaxation itself. In other words, rest "as it is" means to rest in the awareness that always is, as in the awareness it takes to read this. Rest in this awareness that it takes right now to read this sentence, rather than the content (what it means) of this sentence. If you don't know how or if you are currently meditating but not getting the results you hoped for, you can learn to do it right. That is the idea.

Meditation Hurdles

One of the potential problems with learning meditation is that it takes time and practice. Few people have enough time and fewer yet like to practice. A chief hurdle for many folks is finding enough time in a day to practice. Meditation, like any technique, has to be practiced until it becomes almost second nature. For most this involves setting aside some time each day (or every day or so) to practice meditation.

For those of us with busy schedules, often the first thing to get scratched from our daily "to do" list is our meditation practice. Practice of any kind takes effort and spiritual practice has the additional problem that we really have no idea (yet) of what the results or outcome of the training is or will be. We are doing this on spec, and this can be discouraging.

These and other obstacles often lead to would-be meditation practitioners giving up and abandoning their efforts to learn to meditate. This is a generalization, but occasional practicing of meditation every day or so for a short time is a difficult way to reach the critical mass necessary for meditation to become spontaneous.

I am not suggesting practicing for a long time each day unless that is joyful to you. Instead, practice many short times. What is even more needed is some way to apply the meditation technique, not just for one-half hour every a day or so, but all the time in whatever we have to do. IMO, that is the ticket.

Practice Places

Typically, learning meditation technique, what is called "practicing," takes place in a quiet place, often a little cushion off in a corner of a secluded room, and so on. That is where the technique is learned until we are fluent and we can stop "practicing" meditation and instead actually begin to just meditate.

Practicing in a special room, on a cushion, when we can get to it for some bit of time each day (or every day or so) is like going to church on Sunday for an hour or and expecting to get into heaven. Of course, every little bit helps, but given all the variables that can intervene, the amount of practice that accumulates may not amount to enough to reach critical mass.

Daily practice is fine, but too often there are several variables that can intervene and short-circuit our efforts. These include not keeping to our schedule. Often what happens on a busy day is that the first thing that gets cut from our schedule is our meditation practice. Runner-up is that we just don't feel like it that day and are sure that "tomorrow" will be a better time to practice, or we don't feel like we know what we are doing or we are not getting any results, etc. The list goes on. In other words, other methods are needed.

Enter "Reaction Toning," a simple technique that can be done all day long during whatever our normal schedule requires and one that accumulates serious amounts of dharma practice at no extra expense in time or concentration.

Karma

The whole idea of "karma" very much relates to meditation practice and I will explain why, and karma is easy to understand. Our every action has a result. This is simple physics. And we have all heard about "good" and "bad" karma, at least from our point of view. The good karma produces results that we like, while the bad karma makes life more difficult for us.

And there is a popular misconception about karma to the effect that karma mainly relates to the kinds of "sins" listed out in the Ten Commandments, like "Do not kill," "Do not steal," and so on. Of course that is "bad" karma, but there is a much greater source of difficult karma, in particular since most of us are not killing and stealing anyway. I call it micro-karma.

Micro-Karma

As mentioned, it is not just the big karma-forming actions (killing, stealing, etc.) that we should watch out for, but rather the myriad of small actions that we habitually do that create the bulk of our "bad" karma and which most folks have no idea they are accumulating. I call this our micro-karma.

The Tibetan Buddhists differentiate between skillful actions (which they call Skillful-Means) and un-skillful actions, those whose result impair or obscure our minds. When we think of skillful means, we think of intentional actions, but the vast bulk of the 'bad" karma we accumulate is "unintentional" only in that we are not aware of it, but it too has intent. Ignorance of this natural law is no excuse for bad intentions.

Chief among our "unintentional" karma are the reactions we have to almost everything all day long. And by "reactions" I mean our knee-jerk reactions, those we apparently cannot control, mostly because we are not even consciously aware of them. Keep in mind that the name "Buddha" means awakened, the one who is aware. Buddhism is the method (and its practice) of becoming more aware.

We react all day long, but are not aware that we are doing so. When we become aware of our reactions, we can learn to respond appropriately to them, instead of just reacting involuntarily. Thus I am distinguishing here between our uncontrollable "reactions" and appropriate responses. And by "reactions" I am not talking about the kind of reaction we have when we place our hand on a hot stove.

Instead, I am speaking here of the myriad of reactions we have based on our personal likes and dislikes, our prejudice, bias, antipathy, aversion repugnance, bigotry, enmity, etc. that we have built up over the years, mostly thanks to our Self.

The Self

I am not going to go deeply into the concept of the Self. I have a whole book on it for those who are interested. Instead, here I just want to sketch out how our self can affect the accumulation of karma by its many attachments, particularly what it does not like. In brief, the Self is a montage of our likes and dislikes that we draw around us like a coat of many colors, only here it is a persona of many attachments, positive and negative.

The Self does its best to pull everything it likes closer and to keep away (at arm's length) everything it does not like or does not identify with. We all know this. Anyway, the Self reacts to all that it does not like and those reactions are recorded like any other event in our mindstream. The problem is that these reactions are so constant and often so intense that they amount to an almost constant accumulation of karma all day long and even in our dreams at night. And the amazing thing is that we are not even aware that this is taking place, so successfully do we ignore it.

The controversial poet and New-Age harbinger Aleister Crowley penned the phrase "To snatch at a gnat, and swallow a camel." This is effectively what we do with the torrent of reactions we record as karma each day. We are unaware of it all and yet it probably is the single greatest cause of "bad" karma that we have.

As they say, "Karma burns twice," first when it occurs and adds to our obscurations and second when somewhere down the line its imprint has to be removed, expunged.

Luckily there is an easy way for us to address this problem and greatly reduce the amount of micro-karma we record and this is "Reaction Toning," also called "Reaction Tong-Len."

Reaction Toning

Reaction Toning is a complete dharma practice, one that can be done (and is best done) off-the-cushion. Best of all, it does not interfere or add extra time to our busy schedule and day. Personally, I do this all day long. And it amounts to a lot of practice getting done, something very few people achieve since they do not have the time. It's Dharma-on-the-Go, so to speak.

And Reaction Toning is easy to learn, something we can do "on the hoof" so to speak. All that is needed is to begin to be aware of our reactions, and there is no lack of opportunity since we react, literally, all day long. What reactions are we referring to? Literally all of them. For example:

The office worker and not-so-friend that suddenly comes round the corner and confronts us, face-to-face. We may try to control our reaction, but just note it. Note the wince and the avoidance we can feel. What is that?

"That" is nothing more than our reaction, regardless of the cause. The cause may be our instinctual dislike for someone who has offended us. But whether they did something to us on purpose or not is not important. We can't control the outer world, but we can recognize our reaction to it and begin to tone that down. As one of my favorite songwriters Seth Bernard penned, "Make friends with the weather." This does not mean we are unmoved by it, but it is very possible to transform knee-jerk reactions into appropriate responses that do not record karma.

To do this requires that we first note the reaction when it occurs and then recognize the reaction as purely our own. Someone else may be causing it, but how we react is totally up to us. So after recognizing we have reacted, we then own it and acknowledge to ourselves that we alone are reacting. This is our reaction. We own it and because of that we can change and modify it. Once we have owned the reaction, that by itself may be enough for it to begin toning down. Eventually we learn to spot it every time it arises until it no longer arises. Instead we begin to respond to whatever input we receive in an appropriate way. Or we may even do a little traditional Tong-Len with it, taking in the worst from outside (from that other person) and sending back out the best in us we can offer.

I find that merely recognizing and owning my reactions is usually enough right there to begin toning them down and de-emphasizing a particular reaction. The more often we do it, the less emphatic (or traumatic) it becomes. We make friends with it.

Imprint or Groove

Our every negative reaction, let's say to a person we don't like, deepens the groove or trace in our mindstream connected to them. In other words, repeatedly reacting to someone (or something) negatively etches an ever deeper groove in the mind that not only further obscures our mind, but also that someday will have to be removed if we want a clear mind. Think how long and how often these reactions occur. It is scary.

Multiply this by the thousands of reactions we have each day and you get the picture, a torrent of micro-karma that steadily accumulates to our disadvantage. And this micro-karma is not reserved just for people we react negatively to. Our reactions descend to even finer reactions. For example, we don't like that person's nose, scar, scarf, color, or hat. Those too are faithfully recorded in our mindstream. "No reaction is too small" might be the motto here.

In other words, our daily reactions amount to thousands of tiny razor cuts, moments when we automatically wince, that record themselves as karma in our mindstream.

And the amazing thing is that with just a little work we can tone down and eventually remove those reactions and stop recording so much karma. And the byproduct of that is that our mind gradually clears up and we become increasingly more aware. In other words, this is a method to remove the effects of our "bad" karma and to stop recording it. And that is something to consider.

Another plus is that this technique is not rocket science. Anyone can do it and getting started is as easy as your next negative reaction, which probably will be coming along any second. And unlike many forms of meditation training, we can see and experience our progress with Reaction Tong-Len right away. It is a get-paid-as-you-go practice. As we come to terms with each reaction, we can allow the mind to just rest in the space or gap that appears as we own our reactions and they lessen in strength. We embrace them.

And since the process is pretty much instantaneous, we are not losing any time. In fact, we gain time because we are not embroiled in all the wincing, bobbing & weaving, and dodging that we usually do when we react negatively to something. We accumulate time and awareness as we go along.

As to how this method differs from its big brother Tong-Len, Reaction Tong-Len is all about the Self and does not involve others as so many dharma practices do. The Buddhists are very clear that until we enlighten ourselves, we cannot enlighten others. Reaction Toning is like that old kid's game of Pick-Up-Sticks, gradually removing our own obscurations, one-by-one. And what is being removed through Reaction Toning is just that which separates us from others, all of the harsh criticism, bias, prejudice, etc., which is mostly directed at other people. So, Reaction Toning is about removing the "other" in our own self, which translates to an ever more inclusive embrace of everything "else" -- the end of dualisms.

Sending & Receiving: Tong-Len

Tong-len is a Tibetan Buddhist method everyone would do well to learn whether they practice dharma or not. It is that useful! And it is easy to understand and practice. Equally important tong-len is a practice we can do anytime and anywhere. It is portable.

Tong-len is also known by the name "Sending and Receiving" as well as "Exchanging Yourself for Others, or simply "Giving and Taking." It is similar to the Christian motto "Do unto others as you would have them do unto you," but with tong-len we make the first move. We give. And the Buddhists take it to another whole level. Tong-len helps to develop compassion in an organic and very natural way. And the technique is very simple:

When you encounter another person who is suffering or in pain, you simply breathe in (mentally that is) all of their suffering and pain; you take it on or into yourself and you breathe out all your goodness, kindness, happiness, and good will back into them. In other words, you send all your goodness to them and receive from them all of their pain and suffering. You take this (again: mentally) on yourself. This is considered perhaps the quickest method to seriously increase a sense of compassion and to decrease ingrained selfishness. And this can also be done with any world situation, a plane crash, an earthquake, and so on, anywhere there is suffering. Seeing others in pain and suffering is not the only use for this valuable technique. It also works to clear your own personal obscurations on an item by item basis.

In other words, it works equally well for when you encounter people who are angry at you, irritating you, pissing you off, or whatever. The technique is the same.

You simply breathe in (mentally) all that which is 'other' or different and separate from you in the other person and breathe out and back to them all of the goodness and joy in yourself, whatever you can muster at the time. In other words, you breathe into yourself all of the dark, bad, painful, offensive, and "otherness" and you breathe out all that is good, kind, and happy in yourself. From the Western viewpoint this is counter-intuitive, exactly the opposite of what most of us have been taught, which is to keep the good things close and keep the "bad" things as far away as possible.

In tong-len we send to others (exchange with them) all our well-being, happiness, goodness, and receive from them all of their darkness, sadness, pain, suffering, nastiness, and whatever it is that 'we' have labeled or can label as "other" in them. And we do this again and again and again until some equilibrium is achieved between the two of us in our mind. They (the other person) won't even be aware of this, so don't look for them to change their expression. You are detoxing 'your' fear and reaction to them, not their own to you. Sounds scary, no?

When I first read about this technique I thought for all the world that tong-len was a medieval throwback from the Dark Ages. As an astrologer who counseled others for many years I had been taught by western psychics to do just the opposite to tong-len, to get as far away from other's pain as possible and to not take it on personally. I had been told to always wash my hands in running water after a personal reading and imagine all the pain, nastiness, and what-not that I might have picked up from my client going down the drain with the water. Tong-len is 180-degrees different from that approach and this was at first very hard for me to appreciate and accept. Frankly I wanted to cut and run.

I am glad I did not because this highly-efficient technique is spot-on as an antidote for our western tendency to isolate ourselves from others and brand them as 'bad' or at least separate from ourselves. And tong-len is perhaps the quickest and most direct way to extend our own boundaries to include something else beyond our own skin as in: family, friends…. all those other than ourselves.

Tong-len is also useful beyond those we encounter who are suffering and in pain or who irritate or make us angry. That is just the tip of the iceberg for this technique. People we react to strongly in a negative way aside, tong-len is brilliant as a tool to neutralize whatever confronts us from the outside, whatever we have labeled as different or "other" from ourselves -- everything we have marked as "bad" since our childhood, every attitude we have perhaps unconsciously adopted that separates us from the world around us and send us into a karma- making tailspin every time it appears to us.

All of these are expertly handled with a little tong-len practice. And while proper sitting meditation technique is something that can require time and commitment, most Americans take to tong-len right off. They just "get" the concept straight away and start using it. It is that simple.

In summary, tong-len is an easy technique that can be learned almost at once and that can be used not only on the mediation cushion but anytime and anywhere during the rest of our day. What tong-len effectively does is extend the perimeter of what we consider to be our ourselves outward to include more and more of the outside world, a world that 'we' have labeled as "other" than ourselves or for whatever reason just "bad."

With just a little training in tong-len we learn to

become aware every time we catch ourselves labeling another person as someone to close-off and shut out, and we reverse the process. We accept and take them in, essentially making friends with ourselves, because somewhere along the line we have closed the door on that person, food, attitude, or what-have- you?. Tong-len opens that door again.

And doing tong-len with people is only part of what this technique can handle. Any attitude, prejudice, hatred, fear, competitiveness, jealousy, etc. that we become aware of in ourselves can be neutralized with this technique. Notice that key phrase "that we become aware of," because for tong-len to work we have to focus not on the thing we "hate" or react to and then follow that feeling, but rather we focus on the awareness that here is something that "we" hate or don't like. Got it?

For example, if I hate being called "Mike" instead of "Michael," and you just called me 'Mike," I focus my awareness of my reaction to what you just said rather than what you just said and make sure not to follow the reaction and launch into setting you straight with more emotion than it is worth. In other words, we learn to recognize when something is "other" or pops into our view reactively. We catch our reaction. Rather than react, we drop it, and do tong-len with our own reaction. This type of tong-len also helps to remove our prejudices and obscurations one at a time.

With tong-len we gradually extend the limits of our dislikes and prejudices outward much like when a drop of water strikes the surface of a calm lake, concentric circles open and reach out in ever-expanding rings beyond the drop. We become ever more inclusive.

Neutralizing the separation and otherness between

ourselves and the world around us brings enormous benefits. By ending the isolation and separateness (the so-called labeling and prejudice) we get back all of the energy we have locked in holding on to these prejudices and biases all this time. Better yet, once we have neutralized this labeling, we instantly stop creating all of this difficult karma in our mindstream and that stream begins to clear. Remember that every time we invoke a negative reaction to something, even if it is a legitimate gripe, we dig a deeper karmic track in our own mindstream, one that will take more and more work to eventually neutralize or erase.

It does not matter if we have a 'right' to get mad at whatever or whomever offends or confronts us. What matters is that when we do get mad, we only add insult to the injury we may have received by the imagined (or real) affront, internalizing it and recording it ever deeper in our mindstream. Every hatred, prejudice, bias, fear, and doubt that we have locked up in the world that we imagine as outside us is a reflection of an attitude we maintain inside us. We are the one hurt by it. Each instance takes another little piece of our life energy.

When each bias and attitude is gradualy removed, our mind is clearer and our energy greater. And, as mentioned, we are no longer digging our own karmic grave by endlessly reinforcing the trace or track of that "otherness" in our mindstream. It really is a win/win situation, and it is so easy.

Tong-len is the great equalizer and neutralizer. It is perhaps the first Buddhist mind-practice technique those new to the dharma should consider. When I was introduced to tong-len, it scared the bejesus out of me at first glance. But after trying it even for a short while I recognized it for the powerful antidote from my negative attachments that it is.

Tong-Len: How I Came to Learn It

In a previous article I described Tong-len, the powerful Tibetan Buddhist mind practice for developing compassion and paring the ego down to size, not to mention that it helps to remove the myriad of biases and prejudices we inherit from our society or manage to develop ourselves. Here is the story of how I first encountered tong-len many years ago.

I had met this wonderful Tibetan lama (a rinpoche) during a visit of his to Ann Arbor, Michigan and Margaret (my wife) and I were so moved by that meeting that we had to see him again, Khenpo Karthar Rinpoche lived high in the mountains above Woodstock, New York and it was the dead of winter. In fact it was during those weird bardo-like days after Christmas and before the New Year. We all know those days. My wife and I piled our three kids (at the time) into our little car and began an 800-mile drive across the country in a frigid cold spell. Our youngest daughter was only about one and one half years old at the time and normally we would not take such a young child that far away from home in the bitter cold. But we did. That was how important it was for us to meet this rinpoche again. We knew we could learn from this man and we were hungry for a change in our lives.

It was a long trip that took two days and by early evening of the second day we had reached Woodstock, New York. Darkness had set in and the cold was so intense that then entire front inside windshield of the car was frosted over; I was using a business card to scrape a tiny hole in the frosted glass to peer out of. We were driving up the narrow three-mile mountain road to the Buddhist center. It was slow going and were not sure what we would find when we finally got there. Finally we pulled into a small parking lot outside of a large building that used to be a resort hotel. It had seen better days. This was before the monastery was built, although they were beginning to pour the foundation when winter had set in.

We got out of the car and the little group of us stood huddled by the door and knocking. A high wind on the mountain was blowing sharp as we waited. It was dark and there were no outside lights. At last someone came and the door was opened by a very nice lady; we were invited inside. I guess I should tell you now that we had no appointment. No one knew we were coming. We just had winged it. Even so, the lady (her name was Norvie) was very kind and led us into a small waiting room; she would tell the rinpoche and see if he was available.

I will spare you the whole story of that visit and just cut to the chase to save space here. Suffice it to say that the Rinpoche was very kind, but firm. I wanted to know what I should do in order to become his student. Margaret felt similarly. We liked him that much! And pushy me, because I had been an astrologer and done "spiritual" things for many years, I was hoping to place out of "meditation 101" and get right to the advanced stuff. That tells you how foolish I was. Rinpoche very gently told me that he could see that I had never harmed anyone with my astrology, but that when it came to learning meditation, because I knew little to nothing about it (and had done little to nothing with it so far) that it was best if I started at the very beginning. This, he said, would be the fastest way.

The fastest way? Well, I had to think twice about that because my arrogance was acting up again, but I respected this man so much that I was willing to do just as he said. OK, I would start at the beginning. And now I am getting to the point about Tong-len here.

When we were about to leave, Rinpoche gave us a small book called "The Torch of Certainty" by a high lama named Jamgon Kongtrul Lodro Thaye Rinpoche (1830-1899). Later I discovered this was one of the classic mind- training texts used in the Karma Kagyu Lineage. And Rinpoche pointed out the section on Tong-len for us to consider, the technique I described earlier.

When Rinpoche had said goodbye and was gone we went back outside. In the dark we could see the bare cement walls of the monastery being built and the high winds were whipping the plastic covering that was hanging from the newly poured cement. It was a little eerie and there were no stars out. Anyway, we drove our little car slowly back down the mountain and managed to find a motel in Woodstock where we could stay the night.

There we were, crammed into one room that had a single (and very small) infrared wall heater that barely kept the bitter cold outside where it belonged. Anyway, there with our little kids we opened this small book and began to read the section on tong-len, a technique we certainly had never heard of before. And it was a shocker.

Maybe it was just the night and the fact that we were huddled together around a tiny heater (with our babies) 800 miles from home on one of the most bitter winter nights of that year. What this book said was to breathe into yourself all the darkness and suffering in the world and breathe back out whatever good feeling and well-being you had. In fact the tong-len technique is often simply translated as "Exchanging Yourself for Others."

Well this suggestion went 180-degrees against what every spiritual person and technique had taught me up to that point. In fact, I had been taught to not take in anything dark, negative, or fear-filled, and to keep such things as far away from me as possible. Psychics had even shown me how to wash my hands after doing an astrology reading for a client and let the harmful and negative thoughts that might otherwise accumulate just go down the drain. So tong-len was saying just the opposite and I mean totally the opposite: that I was to breathe in the bad stuff and give others or whatever was out there any good stuff I had. What?

I know Margaret and I looked each other in the eye and wondered what had we gotten ourselves into? It was scary and very hard to get our mind around it. At first my gut feeling was to just cut and run and to get the hell out of there. Yet here we were, shivering together in this tiny hotel room so far from home. There was no instant solution. But we read on. We had nothing else to do.

Gradually we learned that tong-len, despite how it appeared to us at the time, was an advanced shortcut to compassion and the handling of suffering and negativity. All my life I had tried to keep as far away from anything negative (people and things) as I could. I mean: who wants that? And here was a technique telling me to do just the opposite, to welcome and breathe all this bad stuff into me and exchange it in the outbreath for whatever good stuff, feelings, and thoughts I had. These Tibetans get right to the heart every time. It got my attention.

Well, we got through the night, back on the road, and finally made it all way the home and with the concept of tong-len still intact. We would give it a try and we did. So there you have the story of how we came upon tong-len.

Tong-len has turned out to be an incredible and efficient method to remove obscurations and all the mental prejudice that I have accumulated, including those that society had gifted me with by just being born in my particular where and when I did. And unlike sitting meditation, which I found quite difficult to obtain results from, tong-len was easy to learn and do. All it required was that I gradually become more aware of my own negative reactions, biases, and reconceptions. Instead of simply following them as I had all my life, I learned to recognize and neutralize them as they arose using the tong-len technique. I made friends with my own enemies and gradually removed the walls of my personality.

Here I have given you kind of a short-hand introduction to tong-len. It would be best to learn it formally from a teacher, if you can. There are also other considerations that are very important, like making aspirations (intent) before you begin and dedicating the merit of whatever practice you do to benefit all sentient beings, that kind of thing. I have covered those elsewhere in a book called "Dharma: The Intangibles," which can be found as a free e-book here.

http://spiritgrooves.net/e-Books.aspx

Response Ability

I am taking off my story-telling hat and putting on my didactic hat, because I keep running across folks in my life that have managed to paint themselves into one corner or another because they react instead of respond. It makes me want to comment, and I am.

I have been counseling for something like 45 years now, and I want to share with you what I find to be a key factor in that experience. Much of what takes place in a counseling session boils down to how a person responds to what is happening to them in their life. We can't control what others say and do to us personally, much less what happens in the outside world of news events. That is what dictators try to do and they all eventually fail.

And here I am not referring to our own complex inner filters or the neuroses that we ourselves project outside ourselves on the movie screen of life and then intently watch. Rather I am talking about outside events that are actually independent of us and our mental projections, events that we can't help but react to; we do this all the time.

You and I can't control outside events (what happens to us), but we do have a choice in how we respond to these external events. Our ability to respond is what, of course, is called 'responsibility', a quality much valued in this society. Although everyone has some kind of response to life, not everyone is considered 'responsible'. We can try to learn the correct response to an infinite series of possible events or we can learn to be more generally responsible. This is what employers so desperately look for when they are hiring, someone who is responsible, who naturally has the ability to respond to events in a useful fashion. Trust me, they get the promotions!

And I am making the distinction here between responding and reacting. A simple reaction is not enough; we all do that. We cannot help but react to outside events, but it is 'how' we react that determines whether we react in a so-called

'responsible' manner.

Again: we can't control what happens to us in the outside world; we can only control our own reaction, the way 'we' respond to it. In low-level jobs there frequently is an attempt to anticipate every possible event and train the employee how to respond, by rote. Of course, since there are infinite possibilities, that approach can only go so far.

Much better is to find someone with an ability to respond to all situations, someone who is naturally responsible. This is, of course, an employer's dream. So what am I driving at here?

My point is that it is possible to develop our sense of responsibility to the point where we can naturally just respond to events in a useful (responsible) way.

For example, when someone is angry at us and says or does something hurtful or rude, instead of setting off a domino-effect chain-reaction of anger in response, we can learn to consider the source (they are upset or angry) and just respond appropriately. We can't control them, but we can learn to control our reaction and response to them. This is the essence of many dharma teachings, what is called 'skillful means," responding skillfully.

In almost every case, instead of reacting to the rain of problems that life too often presents to us in a defensive manner (protecting ourselves from them), if we could instead receive and just handle them responsibly, it would be so much better.... for us and the outside world.

It is all a matter of awareness, of learning to catch ourselves before we over-react and start to push back, and instead facilitate and respond to incoming events in a useful manner, like not letting life push our buttons. Awareness training is the single most valuable tool I have yet found.

Our awareness is what makes us able to respond; we are aware of the situation. Some people are born more aware and they are naturally responsible. The rest of us can develop our awareness until we become more responsible. Either way, IMO the key to how we make our way through life (career) is our ability to respond.

Reactive Alchemy

Like going to school for a single class or to church only on Sunday for an hour, with that amount of practice we get what we pay for. An hour or so a week gets us an hour or so a week of training, nothing more. Think it through. If we practiced an hour a week on guitar, we would not exactly be the musician we envisioned.

I don't intend this to sound too harsh, but even an hour a day of practice leaves 23 hours to unravel what we have done and generally accumulate karma. Part-time solutions seldom satisfy full-time needs.

I knew early on I needed to spend more time than that on mind training, but who has the time? In truth, it was not only the time, but also the tedium and boredom I often experienced just sitting there struggling with my mind, usually waiting for the clock to run out. It was pretty much self-defeating and I had no idea then that the struggle was a good sign! Dharma practice should not really be clocked. So what's the solution?

Obviously the solution requires more (not less) time spent, but perhaps in short bursts. Most of the great meditation teachers and texts say to do many short sessions rather than one long session. And they say that we should be careful not to overstay a session by pushing it longer than we feel like. Sure, we can push the limits to see if we like it, but if we don't like it, if we want to cut and run, that is not a good sign. In that case we need to regroup. A certain amount of joy, at least enthusiasm, is required to practice dharma properly. So what are our options?

I already mentioned many short sitting-meditation sessions, but that may be difficult to arrange, fraught with scheduling problems and perhaps self- consciousness. What is needed is a method to practice whenever and wherever we are that does not draw undue attention to itself. Fortunately there is a handy and portable solution at hand, your own moment-to-moment reactions.

It was no accident that my Tibetan dharma teacher (with whom I have been working with for 30 years now) did not first suggest that I learn basic sitting meditation (Shamata). Instead he pointed out a technique called Tong-len in a Tibetan text and suggested I might practice that.

Now Tong-len, when done properly, is a complete dharma practice that we can do anywhere and anytime, so it is very portable. And it is a perfect example of Buddhist psychology, which can involve going against what we would think is the usual flow, going counter to what our personal preference might be. Our self is used to always going for the good stuff, getting more of whatever we like, not less, and certainly not giving anything away. It is almost like the prime rule of self is that we can always add more attachments, but never take any of them away. Left to its own devices, self-attachment is cumulative.

But Tong-len looks the ego right in the eye and suggests just the opposite, to give out with the good stuff and take in what we normally would totally avoid, like the suffering and pain of others that we see in this world. With Tong-len practice we send the best that we have in us out to another, and take in all of the pain and suffering that they have on ourselves. This is not something most of us would think to do, right? It is counter-intuitive to our upbringing.

However, in Buddhist psychology Tong-len is an express route to spiritual growth, a complete form of meditation all by itself. And it is a lot easier for westerners to learn than basic sitting meditation. I am not going to say much here about how the whole idea of Tong-len freaked me out when I first read about it. I have told the story several times in blogs, but it sure disturbed me. It was counter to everything I had been taught up to that point. And I am not even going to go into much detail about the practice of classical Tong- len. I wrote about it earlier in this book or you can find it on the web in many places. Pema Chodron is an expert on Tong-len, and what she writes is accurate.

Suffice it to say that IMO Tong-len is tailor-made for Americans and, better yet, we all already kind of instinctively know how to do it. What I want to explain here is a subset of standard Tong-len. But those of you who respond to this idea, by all means learn the classic Tong-len as traditionally taught, because it is very powerful and totally useful. What I present here is but a refinement, but it may be an easier approach for many of us.

I learned this method from my first true dharma teacher, who shared with me a little trick he did with a piece of string. The secret was that you could add on as much string as you wanted, but you could never take any string away that was once   given. At the time I wondered why he would bother with such a trick, but over time I found the profundity in it. And here is the key.

In western psychology the emphasis is often on removing self-attachments by force, often before we are willing to give them up. Deny ourselves, diet, etc. Tong-len (on the other hand) takes the opposite approach. Self-attachment is removed not by limiting our attachments, but rather by expanding what we identify as self until we identify the entire world (and everyone in it) as part of our self. The more our self becomes identified with everything and everyone, the less hold our attachments have on us and they begin to break down and we see through them. There is no more "self and others," because others have become part of our self. What a brilliant solution to an age-old problem! It is worth thinking this through.

In essence, Tong-len is a method to identify that which we don't already identify with, like everything "else" in the world outside ourselves, especially what we positively reject or don't like -- the "them" is not "me" kind of thing. In other words, as I present it here, this form of Tong-len is about pinpointing our reactions and doing something about transforming them incrementally and on the spot. And it is true alchemy that gives a pure result.

Like all mind training techniques, Tong-len depends on awareness to make it work, so it does require that we wake up enough to notice our own reactions, like if we flinch when someone we really don't like walks into the room. That's a reaction. But it does not have to be another person. It can be a thing or an event, like the wince that comes when we remember we have a dentist appointment -- that kind of experience.

If we wake up to our reactions and begin to watch them carefully, we have a chance to identify and make friends with parts of ourselves that we have somehow excluded from what we could call the inner circle of our self. And I am not talking about an isolated event or two a day. If we are aware, we find ourselves reacting almost constantly to all kinds of stuff all day long. These reactions are perfect opportunities for dharma practice and we can't seem to avoid them anyway. They offer a very rich field of opportunity for transformation.

The point I like to keep in mind is that each reaction that we have is recording its karma in our mindstream. Of course karma leaves its mark, but that is not the whole of it. Karma is also a seed that always grows and ripens in the future. Therefore, every time we react negatively to someone or something, we not only lay down a track in our mindstream, but we reinforce (or underline) that mark by repetition and guarantee that this very thing we try to push away from us will reappear in a larger and stronger version down the line. That is just how it works. And karma grows exponentially, not linearly.

So "reactive Tong-len" is the practice of becoming aware of what we react to, making friends with it, and eventually no longer recording that particular reaction as karma that will (literally) haunt us down the line. If you want to remove the accumulation of loads of karma, monitoring your reactions as described here is a good way to go. And it is so portable. We can do it on or off the cushion, anywhere we are, and all the time. It adds up to real practice beyond what we might otherwise be able to do. And the best thing is that no time is wasted. This may perhaps be the perfect post-meditation dharma practice.

Now I am sure to get a comment or two that this method is all about us, and very selfish on our part, just freeing ourselves from recording more karma. What about helping other people? The answer is very simple. Certainly any person that you make friends with in your mind, that you used to dislike, benefits from your practice. And until we deconstruct the self and its attachments, until they are transparent, we will never gain greater clarity.

And my Buddhist teachers have always encouraged me to first become less attached myself and then try to help others, and not vice versa. Instead, the accent is always on our own practice until such time as we free ourselves and become clear enough to actually be of use to others, and not to just muck things up more than they already are.

Anyway, I have found that monitoring my reactions, recognizing what I am habitually excluding or find negative, and then soothing or making friends with that part of myself is enormously beneficial. And it is portable and easy to do. And best of all, once we identify with our negativities and neutralize them, we no longer record that particular karma. Clarity improves.

Sometimes it is good to start small and work outward, like dropping a pebble in a still pond. As with the "string trick" mentioned earlier, "if you can't beat em', join em'," meaning: if we can't remove our attachments by attrition, try expanding what we include as our self by identifying our negative reactions, making friends with them, and including them as part of who we think we are. It is like blowing up the balloon of the self until it bursts of its own accord by inclusion instead of denial.

Is this not worth trying?

Michael Erlewine
November 18, 2014
Michael@Erlewine.net